PAINTING &
DECORATING
TABLES

PHILLIP C. MYER

NORTH LIGHT BOOKS
CINCINNATI, OHIO

A NOTE ABOUT SAFETY

Due to the toxicity concerns, most art and craft material manufacturers have begun labeling their products with proper health warnings or non-toxic seals. It is always important to read a manufacturer's label when using a product. Follow any warnings about not using the product when pregnant or contemplating pregnancy, about keeping the product out of reach of children or about incompatible products. Always work in a well-ventilated room when using products with fumes.

The information in this book is presented in good faith, but no warranty is given, nor results guaranteed, nor is freedom from any patent to be inferred. Since we have no control over physical conditions surrounding the application of products, techniques and information herein, the publisher and author disclaim any liability for results.

Painting & Decorating Tables. Copyright © 1997 by Phillip C. Myer. Manufactured in China. All rights reserved. No part of this book may be reproduced in any form or by any electronic or mechanical means including information storage and retrieval systems without permission in writing from the publisher, except by a reviewer, who may quote brief passages in a review. Published by North Light Books, an imprint of F&W Publications, Inc., 1507 Dana Avenue, Cincinnati, Ohio 45207. (800) 289-0963. First edition.

Other fine North Light Books are available from your local bookstore, art supply store or direct from the publisher.

01 00 99 98 97   5 4 3 2 1

Library of Congress Cataloging-in-Publication Data

Myer, Phillip C.
    Painting & decorating tables / Phillip C. Myer.
        p.   cm. — (creative finishes series)
    Includes index.
    ISBN 0-89134-769-0 (pbk : alk. paper)
    1. Furniture painting. 2. Texture painting. 3. Table. 4. Decoration and ornament. I. Title. II. Series.
TT199.4.M945   1997
745.7′23—dc21
                                     97-3071
                                     CIP

Edited by Julie Wesling Whaley
Production edited by Marilyn Daiker
Designed by Sandy Conopeotis Kent
Cover photographs by Michael LaRiche

North Light Books are available for sales promotions, premiums and fund-raising use. Special editions or book excerpts can also be created to specification. For details, contact: Special Sales Manager, F&W Publications, 1507 Dana Avenue, Cincinnati, Ohio 45207.

METRIC CONVERSION CHART		
TO CONVERT	**TO**	**MULTIPLY BY**
Inches	Centimeters	2.54
Centimeters	Inches	0.4
Feet	Centimeters	30.5
Centimeters	Feet	0.03
Yards	Meters	0.9
Meters	Yards	1.1
Sq. Inches	Sq. Centimeters	6.45
Sq. Centimeters	Sq. Inches	0.16
Sq. Feet	Sq. Meters	0.09
Sq. Meters	Sq. Feet	10.8
Sq. Yards	Sq. Meters	0.8
Sq. Meters	Sq. Yards	1.2
Pounds	Kilograms	0.45
Kilograms	Pounds	2.2
Ounces	Grams	28.4
Grams	Ounces	0.04

Dedication

I would like to dedicate this book to
my business partner, Andy Jones.
His artistic collaborations continue to inspire
me and push my art to grow and develop.

SPECIAL THANKS

Thanks and gratitude go to the individuals who have worked on this book with me. Special credits go to a superb photographer, Michael LaRiche, who has captured all the stages of the techniques taught in this book plus put my finished artwork in its best light. Many thanks go to the staff at North Light Books: David Lewis, director of North Light; Greg Albert, senior editor; Julie Wesling Whaley, editor; Sandy Conopeotis Kent, book designer.

ABOUT THE AUTHOR

Phillip C. Myer has been painting for over twenty-five years. He is the author of *Creative Paint Finishes for the Home*, *Creative Paint Finishes for Furniture* and *Painting & Decorating Boxes* (North Light Books) as well as ten softcover books on tole and decorative painting. A member of the Society of Decorative Painters for more than twenty years, Phillip teaches seminars across the United States and

at his Atlanta-based studios. Phillip and his business partner, Andy Jones, create custom-painted furniture and interior decorating through their business, PCM Studios.

TABLE OF CONTENTS

INTRODUCTION

*F*inding and creating the right table can provide the "missing link" to the interior decorating projects in your home. Most often, a small side table is the missing piece in a room. Think about it. . . . Haven't you always wanted to fill that open spot or niche in various rooms throughout your home? You are probably in need of a table in a foyer to catch keys and mail, one next to a chair in the family room for drinks, a table in the sunroom for a plant, one in the breakfast room to hold extra serving dishes, a table in the kitchen for the phone, or a table next to your bed for books and a reading lamp. A simple thing such as a decorated table fills a great need throughout your home.

The techniques taught in this book range from very novice-friendly to ones that will take some time and practice to gain the proper skills to achieve the effect. But if you believe in a little extra hard work, patience, practice and—the most important key—a positive attitude at all times (even when problems pop up), I'm sure you'll achieve successful results.

Begin with an old discarded table you have in the basement, garage or attic. You can transform just about any old relic or turn an unfinished table into a real gem that will shine in your decorated room. If you are unsure of what technique and colors to use, experiment on sample boards (old pieces of wood or illustration board). These samples will become keys to open the world of potential ideas for the decorated tables in your home. Good luck, and always remember to enjoy yourself while working on your table projects. ❧

Phillip C. Myer

Before You Begin

*T*here are a few things to familiarize yourself with before beginning to decorate tables. Knowledge and organization are the keys to successful results when executing the techniques taught in this book. Take the time to read thoroughly the next few pages to review the general tools used, basic techniques, brushstrokes and brush loading, as well as transfer, preparation, trimming and finishing methods. Although each project in this book is a self-contained unit featuring the necessary supplies and step-by-step illustrations and instructions, the following "foundation" material will get you started down the right road.

PAINTS AND GLAZES

The house paint coating, art material and craft supply industries have begun the strong movement toward developing and manufacturing environmentally friendly, water-based and water-cleanup products. These products are nontoxic, have little to no odor, and clean up easily with soap and water. The projects found in this book are executed mostly with these environmentally friendly products.

Acrylic Paints

To create your own color mixtures in small quantities, a set of artist's grade or student grade acrylic paints in true artist's pigments will prove useful. I've used Prima Acrylics in the following colors to create a good, basic palette: Cadmium Yellow Medium, Cadmium Orange, Cadmium Red Light, Bright Red, Ultramarine Blue, Alizarin Crimson, Phthalo Green, Leaf Green Light, Leaf Green Dark, Raw Umber, Burnt Sienna, Burnt Umber, Titanium White, Metallic Gold, Iridescent White, Iridescent Gold and Mars Black. By combining these basic colors, you can create any color you need.

Latex Base Paints

You'll need to have a selection of base paints (base coats) to provide the foundation for the paint and craft techniques. Following instructions for each technique, you'll use either a flat or semigloss latex base paint. You can have these colors mixed at a hardware store or home improvement center. Today, most house paint departments have the capability to complete computer color matching. They can match any reference material you bring them (fabric, wallpaper or carpet). For the table projects in this book, a quart (1 liter) of base paint will be more than enough. If you would like to purchase less base paint, an arts-and-crafts store can provide 2-ounce (60ml), 8-ounce (250ml) or 16-ounce (500ml) quantities, but you won't be able to receive custom color matches.

Acrylic Glazing Medium

Many of the table projects require the use of a colored glaze. You can create this colored glaze mixture by adding artist's acrylic or latex house paints to a clear glazing medium. You can buy many ready-made clear glazing products on the market, or you can create your own. You want a glaze product that has an open time (working time) sufficient to manipulate the wet glaze and paint in the desired technique. Due to the size of these table projects, you'll require at least fifteen to twenty minutes of open time to achieve successful results.

You can make your own clear acrylic glazing medium by mixing water-based polyurethane varnish plus acrylic retarder plus water. Place equal amounts of these three products in a jar and stir thoroughly. You'll use this mixture as the base glazing medium to which artist's acrylic colors or house paints are added to create a transparent color glaze.

Ready-Made Colored Glazes

You can also find a selection of ready-made pretinted colored glazes. These products require no mixing or measuring, and are ready to use from the jar. I've used Anita's Faux Easy Glazes for many of the colored glazes found in this book. There are twenty-four colors in the collection and these colors can be intermixed to create new custom colors.

MATERIALS
Decoupage Glue and Craft Glue

To complete the gluing steps found in several techniques, a decoupage

You'll need to gather an assortment of tools and materials to decorate the tables in this book. These basic supplies will create a "creative tool box."

glue and craft glue will be required. A decoupage glue is a white glue with a very thin consistency. A glue that is extremely thick will not work for paper adhesion methods for decoupage. You can take a white craft glue that is somewhat fluid, and thin it down with additional water to a flowing consistency. A craft glue that is thick and creamy in consistency is used for gem adhesion.

Water-Based Varnishes

Water-based polyurethane varnishes are used throughout the techniques found in this book. Polyurethane water-based varnish, such as Anita's, provides better durability, broad open time, and water and alcohol resistance compared to standard acrylic water-based varnishes. You may choose a satin, semigloss or gloss varnish to provide variety to your finished tables.

Fragile Crackle Varnishes

This two-part product system creates a cracked or crazed pattern over the surface. These are clear varnish-like products that react to themselves and can produce a crackle finish over any type of surface.

Spray Finishes

Spray finishes are manufactured in several forms. Today, there are environment-friendly sprays. Spray finishes are available in acrylic-based products for clear, sealing protection or for coloring. Choose satin, semigloss or gloss sheen levels to coat the tables.

BRUSHES

As you build your technique repertoire, you can also build your brush collection. There are several brushes which are considered "workhorse" brushes that are listed in the supplies of just about every technique. These brushes will get used over and over, but if you take care of them, they will last a long time. All brushes listed here are produced by Silver Brush Limited.

Base-Coat Bristle Brush

This is a 3-inch (7.6cm) brush made of natural hairs. The brush hairs are cut at a taper angle to form a sharp, chisel edge. This edge allows you to stroke a straight line; control base paint application; work the brush into tight spots; and stroke on a smooth, even base coat.

Glaze Brush

The glaze brush is two inches (5.1cm) wide and made from soft, natural hairs. This brush is made like the base-coat brush with a tapered cut. The natural hairs soak in sufficient amounts of glaze when loading to allow you to stroke a fair amount of colored glaze onto the surface. Synthetic-hair brushes do not allow you this control because the artificial hair cannot drink in moisture.

Varnish Brush

A 1-inch (2.5cm) brush made of natural hair gives you great control when loading on a water-based varnish. The hairs drink in the varnish, then release it when you apply pressure to the brush. This size brush lets you get varnish into tight recessed areas.

Flogger Brush

This style brush is made of a combination of natural and synthetic hairs that measure five inches (12.7cm) in length beyond the metal ferrule. This brush produces unique marks in the wet paint glaze. The long hairs can create strie, flogging and dragging techniques.

Blending Softener Brush

This brush is made from soft, natural goat hair. Available in 1-, 2- and 3-inch (2.5cm, 5.1cm and 7.6cm) sizes, it is needed for fine blending techniques. The soft hairs of this style brush allow you to move paint and blend with great ease.

Silver Mop Brush

The mop brush is made of soft, natural hairs. A size no. 14 allows the same techniques as the blending softener brush, but enables you to get into specific areas to control the blending techniques.

Golden Natural Flats

You'll need flat brushes in a range of sizes to complete detail work—nos. 8, 12 and 16. These brushes are made from a combination of natural and synthetic hairs. They have sharp, chisel edges to access really specific areas. They can also paint a clean, sharp edge or line on a surface.

Golden Natural Round

A no. 4 round brush is a fine pointed brush used for detail and cleanup work. Made of natural and synthetic hairs, it will hold a good deal of paint.

Golden Natural Script Liner

A script liner in a no. 1 size will allow crisp line work. A script liner differs from a standard liner brush by the length of its hairs. A script liner brush's hairs are about ½" (1.3cm) to ¾" (1.9cm) longer. This extra hair length holds more paint and creates a longer detail line.

Wash Brush

A wide brush in a ¾" (1.9cm) size. Made of a mixture of natural and synthetic hairs that load and release paints, glazes and mediums in a fluid motion.

Foam Brushes

Polyfoam brushes (sponge brushes) in 1-, 2- and 3-inch (2.5cm, 5.1cm and 7.6cm) sizes are ideal for trim, some base-coat painting and applying glue. Do not use them for varnish application; a natural-hair varnish brush provides better results.

TOOLS

The following tools are used in various techniques throughout this book. Refer to the supply list found with each technique to determine what you need.

Tracing Paper

Transparent tracing paper in pad form (12" × 16" [30.5cm × 40.6cm]) or roll form (24" [61cm] long) will be used for tracing and drawing pattern design.

Palette Knife and Paint Stirrers

A palette knife with a long, wide blade is required to thoroughly mix the paint and glaze mixtures. The blade should also be flexible. Wood paint stirrers are needed to mix quarts of paint.

Wax-Coated Palette and Styrofoam Plates

The palette (12" × 16" [30.5cm × 40.6cm] with wax coating) and the Styrofoam plates (with no divided sections) will provide you with surfaces to mix small amounts of acrylic/latex paint and acrylic colored glaze.

Metal Rulers

Rulers in 12" (30.5cm) and 36" (91.4cm) lengths with a corked backing to raise the edge of your work surface will be used for measuring and for ruling-pen work.

Ruling Pen

A ruling pen can be filled with thin-consistency paints to draw on a fine trim or detail line. It has a slot area for filling with paint and a turn screw to adjust line width.

Craft Knife (X-Acto No. 11)

A craft knife with a sharp blade will come in handy for cutting and scoring surfaces.

Brayer

A rubber base brayer can be used to roll over a surface and apply pressure to smooth out an area. It is very handy for laying down decoupage prints and sections of paper.

Credit Card

A credit card can be used as a burnishing tool. With its hard plastic edge, it is good for rubbing down the edge of tape when masking out an area to paint. A tip of a large metal spoon will provide similar results.

Tapes

Several types of tape are required when painting. They should all be repositionable, allowing you to pull up the tape without harming the coating below. Both 3M's white safe release tape and blue long mask tape provide good results. Easy Mask's brown painter's tape is wider, providing broader coverage and protection. And it has adhesive only along one half of the tape to minimize the risk of pulling up paint when you remove the tape.

Sandpaper

A variety of sandpaper in grades of coarse, medium, fine and ultrafine (#400 and #600) will be required to smooth out or distress the surface.

Miscellaneous Items

The following items are some standard household and painting workshop tools. Many are considered tools "that go without mentioning"; that is, they may not be listed in each project in the book. For example, if you are using a quart of paint, you'll need something to open it up with—a paint key.

- Paint key
- Dead pen or stylus
- Pencils
- Erasers
- Toothbrush
- Hammer

- Plastic gloves
- Kitchen sponge
- Cotton rags
- Cheesecloth
- Household plastic wrap
- Bar soap
- Murphy's Oil Soap
- Turpentine
- Acetone
- Paper sacks
- Paper towels
- Facial tissues
- Clear acrylic spray
- Drop cloths
- Sanding block
- Wood putty
- Spackling compound
- Putty knife
- White stain blocking primer
- Paste wax
- #0000 steel wool
- Acrylic retarder
- Containers—small and large butter tubs
- Tack rag
- Gray graphite paper
- White transfer paper

THE BASICS

here are a few basic principles that apply to most of the projects you'll be working on when decorating tables. Read the following information to prepare yourself for the painting adventures that lie ahead.

STAINING

Some of the table projects require staining before decorating and embellishing steps can begin. Staining is quite easy to achieve on an unfinished surface. Dip a cotton rag into a stain or glaze mixture and begin rubbing color on the wood surface in the same direction as the wood grain. Continue to dip the rag into color and rub into the surface until an even coverage is achieved. For darker staining, you can brush on stain/glaze with a glaze brush, then wipe off the excess with a rag.

PRIMING AND PREPARING

Before tables are decorated with paint or covered with paper or fabric (excluding tables that have been stained) they require a coat of primer to seal the surface and create a "tooth" for good adhesion. A white, stain blocking primer, such as KILZ - 2, provides a solid foundation for wood and papier-mache surfaces. Apply one to two coats, lightly sanding when dry.

BASE COATING

An important step in the process of decorating a table is applying a base paint to the surface. It is critical that this foundation color go on in a smooth fashion. To achieve a good, smooth and even base-coat coverage, you should follow a few easy tips. Always load the base-coat bristle brush with plenty of paint, saturating the bristles with color, then lightly stroke the brush's bristles across the side of the paint container. You only need to coat from the chisel edge of the brush up the bristles about one to two inches (2.5 to 5.1cm).

Once the brush's bristles are loaded with paint, begin stroking color on the surface. Tackle one section of the table at a time. Apply paint into all recessed trim areas first, then proceed to the larger span areas. Always stroke in long, fluid strokes—short, choppy strokes make for a messy looking base coat and can be magnified when decorative treatments are placed over them. Apply one coat and let dry thoroughly. Follow the drying schedule found on the paint label. If you do not allow proper curing time, the next coat can sag and cause curtaining.

CLEANING BRUSHES

Once you have invested in good quality brushes, it is important to take care of them. If you will not be using a brush for a period of time and it has paint and glaze in it, you should stop and clean it. Water-based products dry fairly rapidly even when mixed with retarders. So when you are done painting a section, place the brush in a container of water, and when done for the day, take your brushes to the sink and wash them thoroughly with soap and water. Murphy's Oil Soap cleans the acrylics and glazes out of your brushes. Rinse the brush and wash a second time to ensure that all traces of color have been removed from the brush's hairs. The hairs of the brush go much farther past the metal ferrule and you want to remove any paint that may be residing there. Shake off excess moisture and allow to dry.

If for some reason you've allowed acrylic to dry in the brush's hairs, a small amount of acetone will work some or all of the dried acrylic out of the hairs. Note that the acetone may be harsh and harmful to certain types of brush hairs.

SIDE LOADING

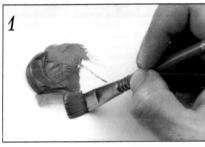

To side load a brush means to carry one color on one half of the brush. The paint is loaded in such a manner that it softly blends away on one side with a crisp color line of definition on the other. Begin by dipping the brush into the painting medium (water for acrylics), blotting on a paper

towel, and stroking one half of the brush along the pile of paint. Move the brush to a new area on the palette and stroke in short pull strokes, blending the color into the medium until there's no discernible definition of where the color stops and the medium begins.

DOUBLE LOADING

To double load a brush means to carry two colors on the brush side by side, with a smooth blend in between. It's easier to double load a flat brush. Make two piles of paint mixed with medium to a thick, creamy consistency. Flatten the piles with a palette knife to form a clean, low edge to stroke up against. Begin loading one half of the brush with the lighter color. Stroke both sides of that half of the brush through the paint. Now, stroke the other half of the brush along the darker color. Move the brush to a new area on the palette. Make short pull strokes to blend the

two colors together in the center of the brush. Restroke along each pile of paint and blend until the brush is saturated.

PAT BLENDING

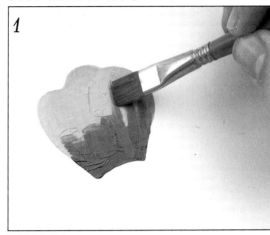

Pat blending softens one color into another but visible brush marks are left on purpose. Pat blending is used for creating effects such as vein sections on leaves. Place two colors side by side and do some quick brush blending.

Now, start at the darkest or lightest point and stroke a series of pull strokes, one overlapping another to form streaks. The streaks can stay consistent in width or change from small to large or large to small. The streaks can also stay straight or curve to create movement. Continue pat blending from one color into another until you achieve a smooth transition.

COMMA STROKE

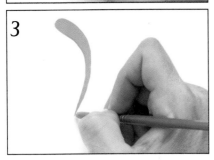

The most recognizable brushstroke is the comma stroke. It is the most important brushstroke to master, for it develops total brush control. Load the brush with paint. Holding the brush at an angle, touch it to the surface and apply pressure to form the head of the stroke. As you begin to release pressure on the brush, curve the brush to the right or left, bringing it up to form a tail to the stroke. When using a round brush, twirl the brush slightly as you lift it up, forming a point with the bristles that will form the tail of the stroke. When using the flat brush, angle the brush upward, making a chisel edge to form the stroke's tail.

S STROKE

The S stroke forms a shape similar to an S. Load the brush with paint. Holding it at an angle, draw a line

stroke. Curve the brush to the right; apply pressure, dragging the brush to form a pull stroke. Begin to lift up on the pressure, curving to the left to form another line stroke at an angle.

A backwards S stroke can also be completed by reversing the direction of the strokes just described.

U STROKE

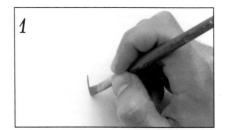

To form the U stroke, load the brush with paint. Stand the brush on its tip and drag it downward to form a line. As you reach the bottom, apply pressure to the brush while curving the brush upward. Pull the brush back up to form a line stroke going upward.

TRACING AND TRANSFERRING

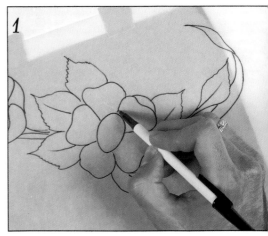

Some of the table projects require the use of a design to follow as a guideline. To use the designs given in this book or to pick up designs elsewhere, you'll need to first carefully trace the design's basic outline by placing tracing paper over the design and going over the lines with a pencil or fine marker. Next, tape the traced design in place with several small pieces of tape. Depending on the background color, you'll slip either gray graphite paper (for light backgrounds) or white transfer paper (for dark backgrounds) under the traced design and go over the basic outline with a dead pen or stylus. Lift the tracing paper up from time to time to see how well the design is transferring.

TRIMMING WITH RULING PEN

A ruling pen can add a fine line of color to a table to trim out the edge or table top. Thin the desired acrylic color with plenty of water. The paint mixture should be quite fluid but have a little body to it. Load a round brush with thinned paint and stroke alongside the ruling pen's open slot to deposit color. Wipe away excess paint on the sides of the pen. Using a cork-backed, raised ruler (so paint does not seep under), hold the pen at a 45-degree angle and stroke alongside the ruler. Complete all parallel lines first, let them dry and then add perpendicular lines.

FINISHING

After you've decorated the table, you want to protect the artwork. Apply at least two coats of a water-based polyurethane varnish over the surface. Use a natural hair varnish brush to flow on a coat of finish. Always be on the lookout for any varnish runs. Allow each coat to dry thoroughly before applying another coat.

For an elaborate finish you can apply a series of three coats of varnish, rub with #0000 steel wool, apply three more coats of varnish, rub with steel wool, apply three more coats, rub with steel wool and apply the last coat of varnish. This will provide you with a "glass-like" look.

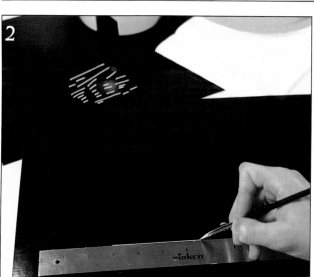

STRIE: LINEAR FINISH

Photo of detail on strie table.

The strie paint finish technique mimics the linear pattern found in strie woven fabrics. This pattern is a color-streaked design that can be made from multiple colors or shades of one color. Although this fabric pattern is made of exacting parallel lines, when this technique is executed with paint and brush, you should expect to see some linear imperfections. A strie paint finish can be created in very subtle looks with base coat and glaze close in value, or high key with great contrast between glaze and base color. ⁊ṧ

TOOLS & MATERIALS

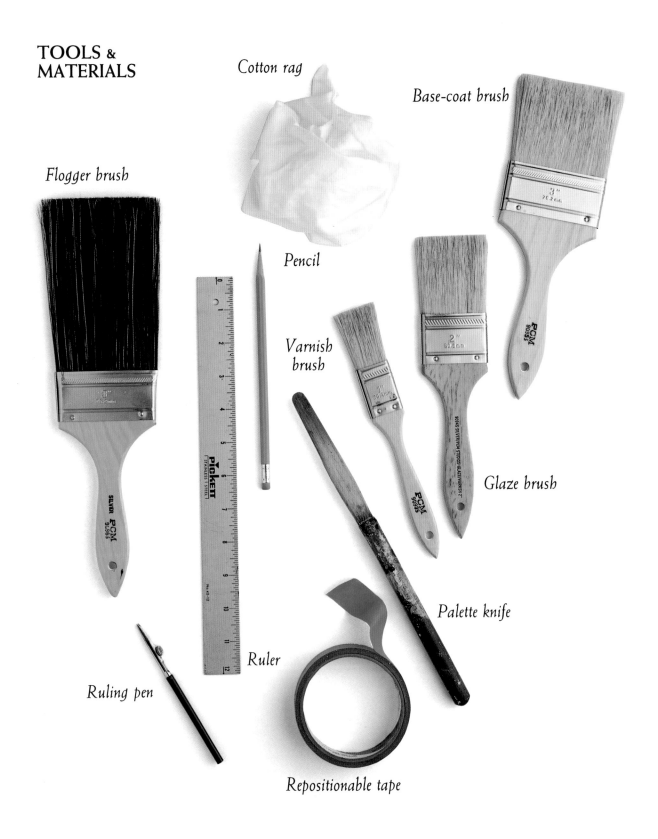

Cotton rag

Base-coat brush

Flogger brush

Pencil

Varnish brush

Glaze brush

Palette knife

Ruler

Ruling pen

Repositionable tape

COLOR CHIPS—ARTIST'S ACRYLIC, WATER-BASED GLAZES, LATEX PAINT

Bright Red artist's acrylic

Dark Williamsburg glaze

Sky Blue semigloss latex paint

White glaze

1 Base coat the table with several coats of Sky Blue (a light blue) semigloss latex paint. Using a base-coat brush, apply smooth, even coats of paint following the direction of the wood grain. Paint the table with coats of paint until an opaque coverage is achieved. Allow each coat to dry thoroughly before applying another.

2 Apply a transparent white glaze to one section of the table surface at a time using a glaze application brush. Brush on glaze in the same direction as the base coat was applied. Try to brush on an even coverage of glaze color so you achieve color value consistency.

3 Lay a flogger brush down on one edge of the table and stroke, applying a fair amount of pressure on the brush. You'll need to stroke in one continuous motion from the starting point to the opposite edge of the surface.

4 Continue to develop the strie pattern on the surface by overlapping the last stroke with the current stroke of the brush. As the brush becomes full of glaze, wipe it on a cotton rag. Allow to dry forty-eight hours before proceeding.

5 For a more advanced look, you can create an inset panel on the tabletop with pencil and ruler. Tape off area with repositionable tape and place a strie pattern with another color. Here, Dark Williamsburg glaze is applied with a 1-inch (2.5cm) varnish brush. After inset is dry, thin Bright Red with water and a palette knife to add ruling pen lines to trim out the tabletop.

DECOUPAGE: VEGETABLE PRINT

Photo of detail on decoupage table.

*D*ecoupage is accented with simple stenciling and a crackle finish to yield a bright, cheerful table for a breakfast room or kitchen. All three techniques executed on this small side table are quite easy to complete, so you can achieve successful results the first time. You can purchase prints that have been reproduced solely for decoupage techniques or locate a print of your own. Instead of cutting out individual pieces, an entire print was adhered to the surface for quick results. A checkerboard stencil trims the side of the print, and a crackle finish covers the entire surface. ❧

DECOUPAGE: VEGETABLE PRINT

TOOLS & MATERIALS

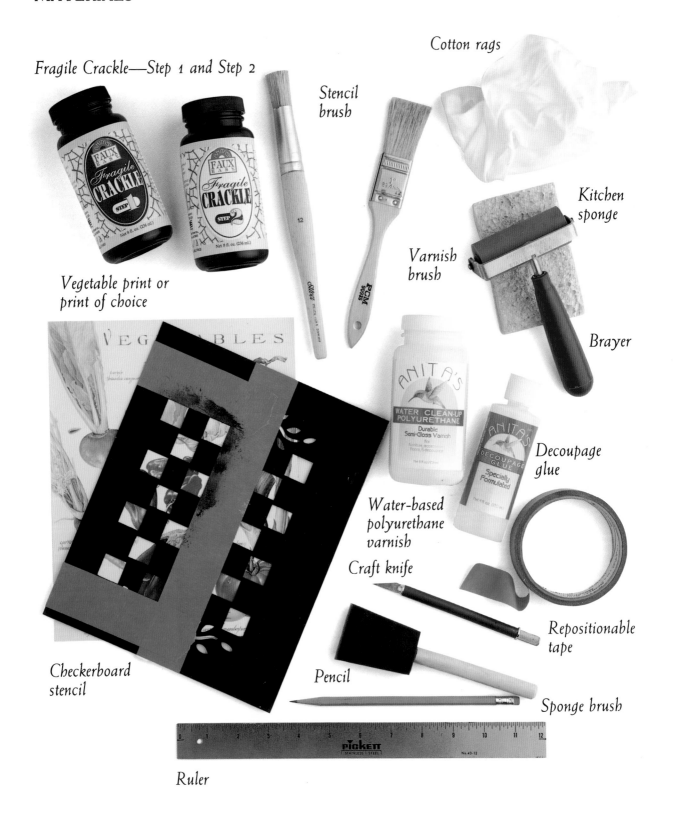

Cotton rags

Fragile Crackle—Step 1 and Step 2

Stencil brush

Kitchen sponge

Varnish brush

Brayer

Vegetable print or print of choice

Decoupage glue

Water-based polyurethane varnish

Craft knife

Repositionable tape

Checkerboard stencil

Pencil

Sponge brush

Ruler

COLOR CHIPS—SPRAY PAINT, WATER-BASED GLAZE, ARTIST'S ACRYLIC

Bright red flat spray paint

Black glaze

Mars Black artist's acrylic

1 Apply a bright red paint to the table using a spray product. The spray paint will yield a superb flat finish that aids in the smooth adhesion of the decoupage print. Hold can about ten to twelve inches (25.4 to 30.5cm) from surface and, in a swiping motion, move across the surface. Avoid runs by applying several light coats rather than one that is heavy.

DECOUPAGE: VEGETABLE PRINT

2 Cut print with craft knife and a ruler. Position print in desired location on tabletop. Measure and mark placement with light pencil lines. Brush decoupage glue on tabletop and on back of print with a sponge brush. Quickly place print on surface and begin smoothing out with a moist kitchen sponge and a brayer. Let dry.

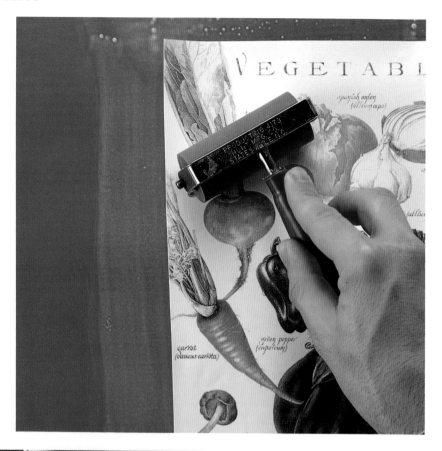

3 Measure and mark area to receive checkerboard design. Tape stencil in place and load the stencil brush with a small amount of black acrylic. Wipe excess paint off on a paper towel. In a light swirling motion, stroke color into stencil openings. You can apply an opaque coverage (as example) or leave a little of the base red showing through in places.

4 Continue to move stencil down the surface to repeat the pattern. Overlap the last set of checker shapes with the openings at the top of the stencil to ensure good alignment. Load the stencil brush and stroke on color in the same manner as described in step three. Let dry. Seal print with a coat of water-based polyurethane varnish.

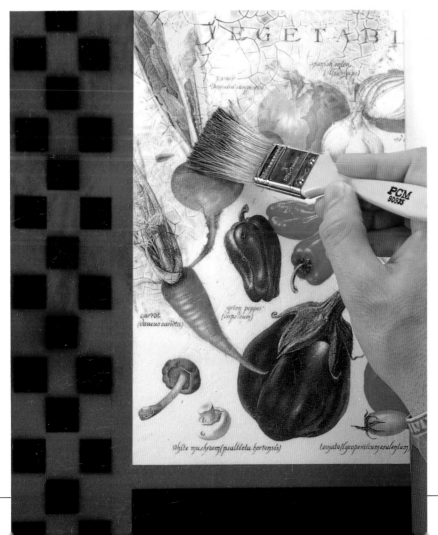

5 To create a crackle finish over the decoupage and stenciling, brush on clear Fragile Crackle Step 1 using a varnish brush and allow to dry. Next, brush on clear Fragile Crackle Step 2. As this dries the crackle pattern will form. To show off these cracks, brush on a transparent black glaze using a glaze brush. Wipe off excess glaze with a cotton rag.

Spray Texture: Pottery Finish

Photo of detail on spray texture table.

This sprayed-on texture creates the roughness found on pottery and statuary pieces. The texture is exaggerated by highlighting it with a piece of sandpaper. This technique can be developed in any color direction you like. Here, a mossy green has been used on a side table which would be perfect for a sunroom or porch. ❧

Hammerite Spray or can paint creates the above fleck – very hard surface.

TOOLS & MATERIALS

Sandpaper, medium and coarse grades

Glaze brush

Tack rag

Mop brush

Pottery Coat

Cotton rags

Base-coat brush

COLOR CHIPS—WATER-BASED GLAZE, LATEX PAINT

Moss Green glaze

Sand semigloss latex paint

1 Base coat the wood table with several coats of a primer using a base-coat bristle brush. Sand lightly between coats with medium sandpaper and remove sanding dust with a tack rag. Allow to dry.

2 To create texture on the surface, spray on several light coats of Pottery Coat. Hold can ten to twelve inches (25.4 to 30.5cm) from the surface and in a swiping motion coat one section of the table at a time. To build up texture, allow texture to dry between coats.

3 Base coat the texture with Sand (a medium-value tan) semigloss latex paint. Use a base-coat bristle brush and be sure to work the paint into texture crevasses. Apply several coats until an opaque coverage is achieved.

4 Load glaze application brush with Moss Green water-based glaze and begin to brush and scrub color into texture. After coating a section of the table with glaze, pick up a cotton rag and wipe off excess glaze in a circular motion. Soften any areas of the glaze by dusting the surface with a mop brush. Let glaze dry twenty-four hours.

5 To highlight texture, place a coarse grade of sandpaper on a sanding block or hold sandpaper flat on surface with your hands. Stroke over the surface with sandpaper to remove glaze and base coat, spotlighting the texture's peaks. Remove sanding dust with a tack rag.

DECORATIVE PAINTING: STRAWBERRIES

Photo of detail on strawberry table.

This whimsical style of decoratively painted strawberries has been rendered in a method that a novice will have success with the first time. The blending method employed here is a loose, visual color blend versus a smooth brushstroke blending technique. The illusion of dimension and form of the strawberries is achieved through the dabbing on of color values in decreasing sizes and ascending brightness. This provides an illusion to the viewer (through casual glances at the subject matter) that these dabs of color are actually more formally blended together. ⚘

TOOLS & MATERIALS

Cotton rags

Flat shader brushes

No. 8

No. 12

No. 4 round brush

Toothbrush

No. 16

Facial tissue

Mop brush

No. 1 script liner brush

KRYLON CRYSTAL CLEAR ACRYLIC COATING 1303

White transfer paper

Base-coat brush

Pattern on tracing paper

Glaze brush

Clear acrylic spray

Stylus

Repositionable tape

COLOR CHIPS—ARTIST'S ACRYLICS, WATER-BASED GLAZES, LATEX PAINT

Alizarin Crimson
Bright Red
Cadmium Red Light
Cadmium Yellow
 Medium

Ultramarine Blue
Titanium White plus
 Ultramarine Blue
 plus black
Phthalo Green plus
 black
Phthalo Green

Alizarin Crimson
 plus Burnt Umber
Burnt Umber
Dark Brown glaze
Indian Brown glaze

Mars Black
Titanium White

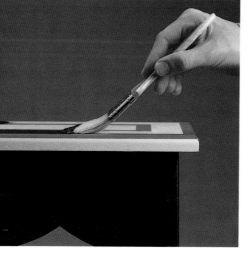

1 Stain the table legs and apron by brushing on black acrylic that has been thinned with water to ink-like consistency. Brush on black stain with glaze brush and wipe off excess with a cotton rag. Base coat the table-top in an off-white semigloss latex paint using a base-coat bristle brush. Let dry. Measure off a 1½" (3.8cm) interior border area. Mask off band with tape and paint it with straight black acrylic and a no. 16 flat brush.

2 Trace and transfer design. Using a no. 12 flat shader brush, base coat the strawberries in Titanium White and allow to dry. Then coat the strawberries with two coats of Bright Red. Base coat the leaves in a mixture of Phthalo Green plus Mars Black. Follow the natural shape of the leaf when stroking on this color.

3 To create dimensional form on the berries, place two oval shapes of Cadmium Red Light on the left side using a no. 8 flat shader brush. To develop shading on the berry, load the no. 16 flat shader brush with a mixture of Alizarin Crimson plus Burnt Umber. Dab this mixture around the calyx and down the center of the berry in a backwards **C** shape. Let dry and apply a second coat.

4 Next place three descending (in size) oval color shapes within the Cadmium Red Light. Place on a mixture of Cadmium Red Light and Cadmium Yellow Medium, then add more Cadmium Yellow Medium to the mixture to lighten, and then straight Cadmium Yellow Medium. Re-coat the leaves with leaf base mixture using a no. 12 flat shader brush. While still wet, overstroke from the edge of the leaf with Alizarin Crimson plus Burnt Umber using a no. 8 flat shader brush. Then, stroke on ice blue mixture (Titanium White plus Ultramarine Blue plus Mars Black) from the outside edge of the leaf.

5 Paint on strawberry calyx with leaf base color mixture and a no. 8 flat shader brush. Highlight the individual calyx section with a side loaded no. 8 brush of ice blue mixture. Paint on two more descending (in size) ovals of color—Cadmium Yellow Medium plus white and then straight white—using a no. 4 round brush. Seeds are painted as dots of color (Mars Black, Bright Red, Cadmium Yellow Medium, Titanium White) by dipping the handle end of the brush in color and hitting the surface. Stroke on veins on leaves with ice blue mixture using no. 1 script liner brush. Brush stroke border in Bright Red using a no. 4 round brush. Let dry for two hours and mist with clear acrylic spray. Antique with Dark Brown glaze and Indian Brown glaze. Brush on with glaze brush, soften with facial tissue and a mop brush. Remove as much or as little of the glaze as necessary to antique the table. Flyspeck with brown glazes and toothbrush.

CERAMIC APPLICATION: BROKEN TILE

Photo of detail on broken tile table.

The combination of whole and broken tile pieces makes for a pleasing and casual contrast on this tabletop. This end table would be ideal for a family room, sunroom, porch or breakfast room. No worries about damaging the tabletop's finish—plants, sweating drinks and food items can't hurt the broken tile finish.

You can coordinate this piece to match the tile found in your kitchen or bathroom, or tie in the decor of several rooms. This technique creates a little mess but the finished results are worth it.

In addition to the tools and materials listed, you'll need flat molding about 1″ (2.5cm) high to create a "lip" around the perimeter of the tabletop. ✑

TOOLS & MATERIALS

Hammer

Brads

Tile trowel

Base-coat brush

Grout in plastic tub

Tile

HENRY
314
non-flammable • latex-based
MULTI-PURPOSE
CERAMIC WALL &
FLOOR TILE ADHESIVE
Type I Formulation
WARNING! SKIN IRRITANT
See Other Cautions on Back Panel
32 FL OZ (1 QT) .946 L

Tile adhesive

Cotton rags

Saw

Kitchen sponge

COLOR CHIP—LATEX PAINT

Mushroom semigloss latex paint

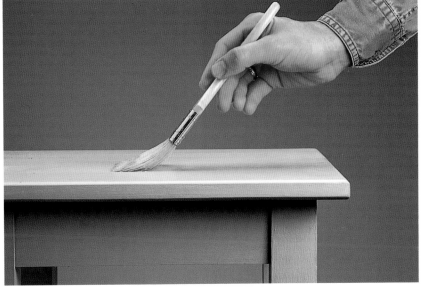

1 Base coat the table in a color to coordinate with the chosen tile grout color, using a base-coat brush. Paint the table with several coats of a semigloss latex paint. Let dry. Trim edges of the table with flat molding about 1″ (2.5cm) high. This will create a lip to hold the tile and grout in place. Nail molding in place and paint it with base color.

2 Using the trowel, stroke an even coating of tile adhesive on the tabletop surface. Stroke over the surface several times with the trowel to create a fine network of grooves. Be sure the adhesive coating is consistent so you can place the tiles evenly.

CERAMIC APPLICATION: BROKEN TILE

3 Begin placing the border of whole 1-inch-square (2.5cm²) tiles into the adhesive. Press the tiles into the adhesive to ensure good contact. Use your eye in placing the tiles about ¼″ (0.6cm) apart.

4 Now, you can begin positioning the broken tile pieces. Break the tiles by hitting them carefully with a hammer. When using multiple colors of broken tile pieces, alternate their placement. After all the tiles are in place, let adhesive dry for twenty-four hours.

5 Mix tile grout with water following the directions on the grout
box. Begin working the grout into the
spaces between the tiles. You can use
your hands, tile trowel or a wood
stick. Remove excess grout and allow
to set up for about fifteen minutes.

6 Moisten a cotton rag with water
and wipe away excess grout.
Then let grout dry (for about forty
minutes) and a haze will form over
the tiles. Use a clean kitchen sponge
moistened with water to clean off
grout haze.

TOLE PAINTING: PENNSYLVANIA DUTCH

Photo of detail on Pennsylvania Dutch table.

This metal table features a traditional Pennsylvania Dutch design of ball flowers and brushstrokes against a dark coppery black background. This style of painting evokes an antique quality mimicking the tole painting of the eighteenth century. The addition of a faux rust technique and antiquing adds to the illusion that this piece of furniture is much older than it is. You control the amount of aging patina (rust and antiquing glaze) that appears on the surface from a light to heavy application. ❧

TOOLS & MATERIALS

Cotton rags

Mop brush

No. 4 round brush

Glaze brush

No. 1 script liner brush

Varnish brush

No. 12 flat shader brush

Sand

Stylus

Pattern on tracing paper

White transfer paper

Red primer spray paint

COLOR CHIPS—ARTIST'S ACRYLICS, WATER-BASED GLAZES

Alizarin Crimson
Bright Red
Cadmium Red Light
Cadmium Yellow
  Medium

Ultramarine Blue
Permanent Green
  Light plus
  Ultramarine
Permanent Green
  Light
Permanent Green
  Light plus
  Cadmium Yellow
  Medium

Alizarin Crimson
  plus Burnt Umber
Burnt Umber
Dark Brown glaze
Indian Brown glaze

Mars Black

1 If you like the overall color of the existing metal table, all you need to do is thoroughly clean the surface. You want to remove any traces of grease or oils that may be on the metal surface. Wash the surface with water and a grease-removing detergent. Let metal surface dry thoroughly before proceeding.

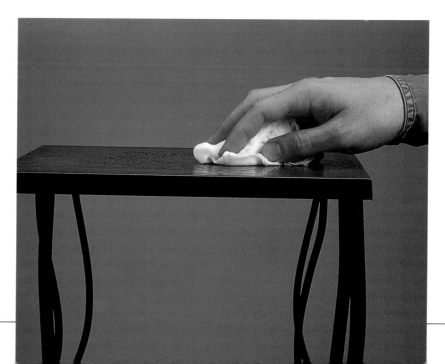

TOLE PAINTING: PENNSYLVANIA DUTCH

2 Trace and transfer the design to the surface using a pattern, white transfer paper and a stylus or dead pen. Base coat the ball flowers in Bright Red using a no. 12 flat brush. Paint the leaflike comma brushstrokes in Permanent Green Light plus black using a no. 4 round brush. Add scrolls in thin-consistency leaf mixture using a no. 1 liner brush.

3 Add four comma strokes of Cadmium Red Light on the right side and four comma strokes of Alizarin Crimson plus Burnt Umber on the left side of the ball flower. Place yellow dots on the ball flowers and near the brushstrokes (in descending sizes) using the handle end of the brush. Place a series of comma strokes descending in size on the leaflike strokes with Permanent Green Light plus Ultramarine Blue and straight Cadmium Yellow Medium.

4 After allowing the paint to cure and dry for two hours, you can create the rust effect by sprinkling the surface with sand. Protect some areas where you wish no rust to appear by applying lots of sand, and leave other areas exposed with very little sand to receive the rust look. Holding can of red primer spray ten to twelve inches (25.4 to 30.5cm) from surface, spray a light misting in a swiping motion. Let spray paint dry with sand in place. Brush excess sand off surface. Note some sand particles will have embedded themselves into the wet paint helping to create the illusion of rust. Seal paint and sand with a coat of varnish using a varnish brush.

5 To antique the surface, brush a mixture of Dark Brown glaze and Indian Brown glaze on the surface using a glaze brush. Using a cotton rag, begin wiping away as much of the glaze as desired. To soften antiquing, dust the surface with a mop brush.

DISTRESSING: WAX TECHNIQUE

Photo of detail on wax distressed table.

*T*oday, distressed effects on furniture are among the most popular paint finishes. Their tactile and casual qualities lend themselves to many types of decorating styles. Here, wax repels the paint, creating irregular patterns. The top layer of paint looks like it has flaked off or peeled away. Like antiquing (see pages 37 and 49), you can control the amount of "aging" on your table surface by using a heavy distressing (with a good deal of wax) to a light application. ❧

TOOLS & MATERIALS

Cotton rags

Glaze brush

Base-coat brush

Furniture wax

Cheesecloth

COLOR CHIPS—LATEX SEMIGLOSS PAINT

Venetian Blue
Venetian Blue glaze
White

1 Base coat the table with several coats of White semigloss latex paint using a base-coat brush. Brush on the paint following the natural grain of the wood. Allow each coat to dry thoroughly before applying another coat.

2 Load a piece of cheesecloth with furniture wax and coat the furniture surface. Stroke or streak on the wax in a linear fashion. Note, wherever the wax is placed, paint glaze will repel. Place wax in areas that would naturally receive wear and tear—edges, corners, around handles or knobs.

3 Thin down the Venetian Blue latex paint with water to a flowing, transparent consistency. Load a glaze brush with the mixture and begin stroking the watery color on the surface. You should see areas that instantly repel and bead up.

4 Continue to add paint glaze to the surface. If you would like an avant-garde look, you can actually let paint glaze run down the vertical surfaces (table legs). This can be achieved by wiping the used brush on a rag, loading with water and stroking over existing paint glaze with water.

5 To create contrast from the transparent paint runs, load the brush with paint straight from the can and stroke on using the chisel edge of the glaze brush. This will help "feather" the more opaque paint into the wet, thin-consistency paint.

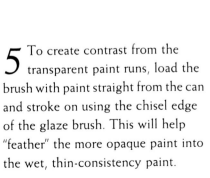

PEN-AND-INK COLOR WASH: VIOLETS

Photo of detail on pen-and-ink violet table.

*S*imple lines of this violet design were drawn on the tabletop with a permanent marker. Transparent color washes were added in a coloring-book style. You don't need great drawing or painting skills to achieve successful results with this method. You can execute this technique with virtually any type of subject matter providing a fairly quick and easy way to render repetitive designs on the table surface. You also have the option to make the pen-and-ink line work as subtle or as bold as you desire.

PEN-AND-INK COLOR WASH: VIOLETS

TOOLS & MATERIALS

Transparent oil color—
Permasols

No. 12 flat shader brush

No. 8 flat shader brush

No. 1 script liner brush

Mop brush

Facial
tissues

Toothbrush

Base-coat brush

Graphite
transfer
paper

Stylus

Clear acrylic spray

KRYLON
CRYSTAL
CLEAR
ACRYLIC COATING
1303

Provides a Permanent
Protective Gloss Coating

DANGER! EXTREMELY FLAMMABLE
CONTENTS UNDER PRESSURE. VAPOR HARMFUL.
IF INHALED, MAY BE FATAL IF SWALLOWED.
Net Wt. 11 oz. • 312 g

Pattern on tracing paper

Permanent markers—
black fine point

COLOR CHIPS—TRANSPARENT OIL COLORS, LATEX PAINT

Permasol Red
  Orange plus
    Permasol Blue Light
Permasol Brown
Permasol Yellow
  Green
White flat latex paint

1 Base coat the table with several coats of white flat latex paint. (A semigloss paint will not work for this technique.) Using a base-coat application brush, apply smooth coats of paint. Allow each coat to dry thoroughly before applying another coat. You want to achieve a pure, opaque white coating.

2 Trace and transfer the violet design to the tabletop using the pattern, stylus and graphite paper. With a permanent black marker go over the basic outline of the violet design. Use a light amount of pressure in order not to expand your line width too much. You can simply outline the design, or for a more advanced look, you can add a small number of crosshatched shading lines. When inking is complete, lightly mist the surface with clear acrylic spray.

PEN-AND-INK COLOR WASH: VIOLETS

3 Pick up a small amount of Perma-sol Brown on one half of a no. 12 flat shader brush and place color around design. Position the strongest amount of color right up against leaves and violets. Work on a small section at a time.

4 Once background brown tones are in place in a section or two, loosely wad up a facial tissue in your hand and in a light circular motion, begin feathering out the color. Blend out color so there is not a great distinction where color stops.

5 To place color in leaves, load the no. 12 flat shader brush with Permasol Yellow Green and stroke on at the base of the leaf. Pick up a mop brush and bounce color outward to the leaf's tip. To highlight the leaf, wipe out color from the center vein on one side of the leaf with a no. 8 flat shader brush.

6 To color violets, make a mixture of Permasol Blue Light plus Red Orange to a shade of deep purple. Stroke a small amount of this color on each violet petal. Pull brush from the outer edge of the petal toward the center. To create highlights, use a no. 8 flat shader brush and wipe out color to expose parts of the white background. Use the liner brush to wipe out "mustache" shapes. Flyspeck the table with toothbrush and Permasol Brown.

DECORATIVE PAINTING: GOOSEBERRIES

Photo of detail on gooseberry table.

The backdrop to the gooseberry and leaf design is a rich, rustic distressed finish. A yellow green base color was applied then distressed with sandpaper to expose the natural wood grain below. A perimeter design of twig branches, flowing leaves and bursting gooseberries creates a "back to nature" look that is so popular today. You also have the option to distress through the decorative painting in a few places for a total beat-up look. This table would be great for the potting shed, greenhouse or any room devoted to horticultural pursuits. ❧

TOOLS & MATERIALS

No. 8 flat
shader brush

No. 1 scrip
liner brush

No. 12 flat
shader brush

Base-coat
brush

Glaze brush

Cotton rags

Graphite
transfer
paper

Pattern on tracing paper

Sandpaper—coarse,
medium grades

COLOR CHIPS—ARTIST'S ACRYLICS

Alizarin Crimson
Burnt Umber
Alizarin Crimson
* plus Burnt Umber*
Cadmium Yellow
* Medium*

Phthalo Green plus
* Ultramarine Blue*
Phthalo Green plus
* Cadmium Yellow*
* Medium*
Cadmium Yellow
* Medium plus black*
Ultramarine Blue

Mars Black
Titanium White

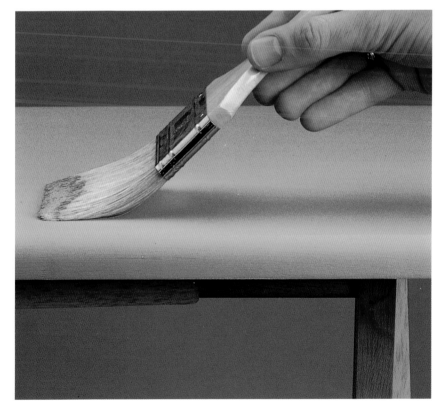

1 Base coat the table in a yellow-green flat latex paint—Cadmium Yellow Medium plus black (or color of choice). Apply several coats until an opaque coverage is achieved using a base-coat application brush. Let paint dry thoroughly. To distress table, with a piece of coarse sandpaper begin sanding through the paint down to the wood below. Distress table's edges and a few places in the center. Smooth out coarse sanding with a piece of medium-grade sandpaper. To soften distressing, thin white acrylic with water and brush on a color wash with the glaze brush. Wipe off excess with cotton rag.

2 Trace and transfer the branch, leaf and gooseberry design to the table surface with tracing paper and graphite transfer paper. Thin down Burnt Umber to inklike consistency with water. Load liner brush with paint and loosely stroke on the twig-like branch structure.

3 Double load a no. 12 flat shader brush with Burnt Umber on one side and Phthalo Green plus Cadmium Yellow Medium on the other. Stroke the Burnt Umber side of the brush at the base of the leaves, down the center vein and where one leaf tucks underneath another. Base in no more than two leaves at a time.

DECORATIVE PAINTING: GOOSEBERRIES

4 Place Cadmium Yellow Medium in the center area of the leaf. Lightly blend the colors of the leaf while they are still wet. A simple pat-blending method will result in the quickest smoothly blended look.

To base the gooseberry, double load a flat shader brush with Phthalo Green plus Ultramarine Blue on one side and Cadmium Yellow Medium plus Mars Black on the other. Stroke on a **C** of dark on the left side of the berry slightly in from the outer edge. Again, base in only a couple of berries at a time.

5 Place white in the center of the berry and Cadmium Yellow Medium plus black in remaining open areas. Pat blend between colors with a no. 8 flat shader brush. Let dry. Place on "ribbed" section lines using a liner brush and thin-consistency white plus Cadmium Yellow Medium plus black and pure white. Add a dot of white for highlight. Gooseberry blossom end is painted in thin Burnt Umber. Add accents to the leaves by side loading a no. 8 flat shader brush in Alizarin Crimson plus Burnt Umber and stroking a small amount of color on the edges and tips of the leaves. Flyspeck the surface with a toothbrush loaded with thin-consistency Cadmium Yellow Medium plus black.

CRACKLING: AGING FINISH

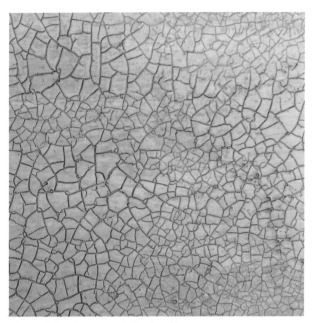

Photo of detail on crackle finish table.

*L*ike distress finishes (see pages 50-55), crackle finishes have gained in popularity due to their casual and tactile nature. An aged patina provides a warm, homespun quality to any table. This technique evokes memories of tables found in Grandmother's barn or garage. These tables were set aside for another day but did not fair well with the changes in climate and temperature that often caused the varnish and paint finish to crack and craze over time. Yesteryear's accident has turned into today's desired finished effect. But you don't have to wait for time and nature's elements to achieve this look—you can simply apply products that have been designed to create this chemical-reaction pattern. ❧

TOOLS & MATERIALS

Step 1

Fragile Crackle—

Step 2

Varnish brush

Glaze brush

Mop brush

Base-coat brush

Cotton rags

COLOR CHIPS—WATER-BASED GLAZES, LATEX PAINT

Dark Brown glaze
Indian Brown glaze
Sand semigloss latex
*   paint*

1 Base coat the table in several coats of Sand (medium-value tan) semigloss latex paint using a base-coat application brush. Apply several coats until an opaque coverage is achieved. Allow paint to dry thoroughly and cure before applying crackle finish.

CRACKLING: AGING FINISH

2 Apply Fragile Crackle Step 1 which is a clear, varnish-like product. Use a natural hair varnish brush. Brush on a smooth, flowing coat stroking in a long fluid motion. Let the surface dry for about an hour—until it's dry to the touch.

3 Apply Fragile Crackle Step 2 using a varnish brush. Apply the second product in a crisscross brushstroke pattern. Coat the surface with a flowing coverage, but don't leave a thick puddle of the product sitting on the surface. Brush out smoothly—cracked pattern will vary slightly. Thin coats of Step 2 create smaller cracks; slightly thicker coats create larger cracks. Cracks will form as Step 2 dries—in about an hour.

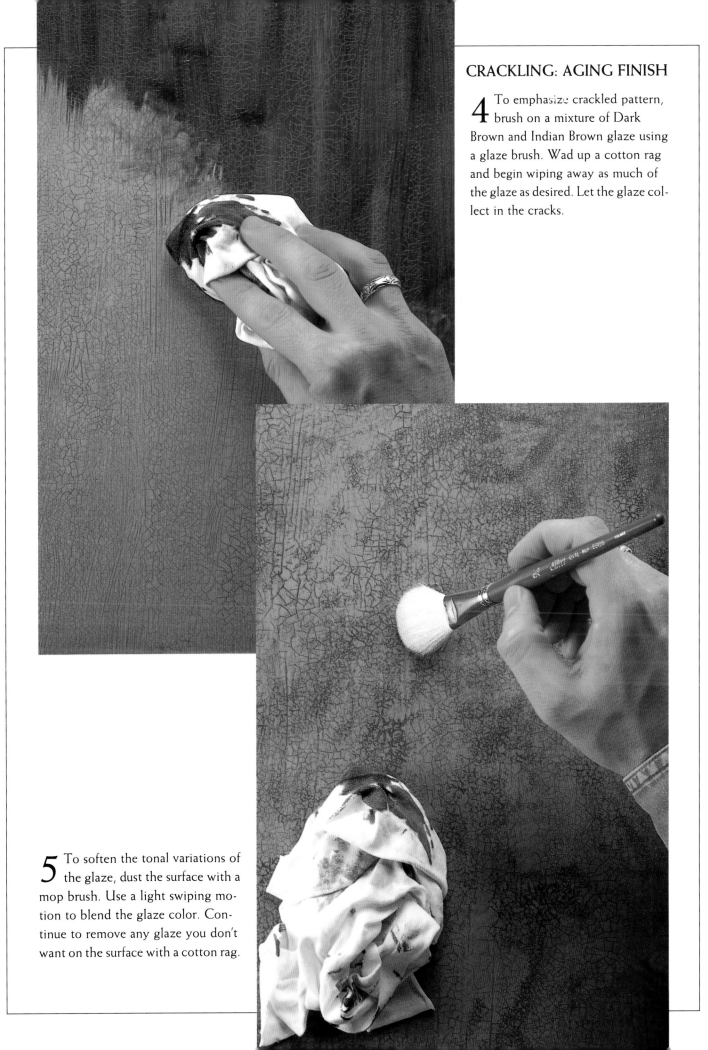

CRACKLING: AGING FINISH

4 To emphasize crackled pattern, brush on a mixture of Dark Brown and Indian Brown glaze using a glaze brush. Wad up a cotton rag and begin wiping away as much of the glaze as desired. Let the glaze collect in the cracks.

5 To soften the tonal variations of the glaze, dust the surface with a mop brush. Use a light swiping motion to blend the glaze color. Continue to remove any glaze you don't want on the surface with a cotton rag.

DECORATIVE PAINTING: ROSES

Photo of detail on rose table.

*P*ainted roses are a traditional favorite. Here, pink roses are painted against a stained finished in a dusty rose tone on a heart-shaped table. This table would be ideal for a feminine bedroom or sitting room decorated in a casual English country style. Learning how to paint stroke roses beautifully will take time and practice. But if you pay your dues by learning how to load your brush and practicing all the individual brushstrokes, you'll have roses blooming from your paintbrush. ❧

TOOLS & MATERIALS

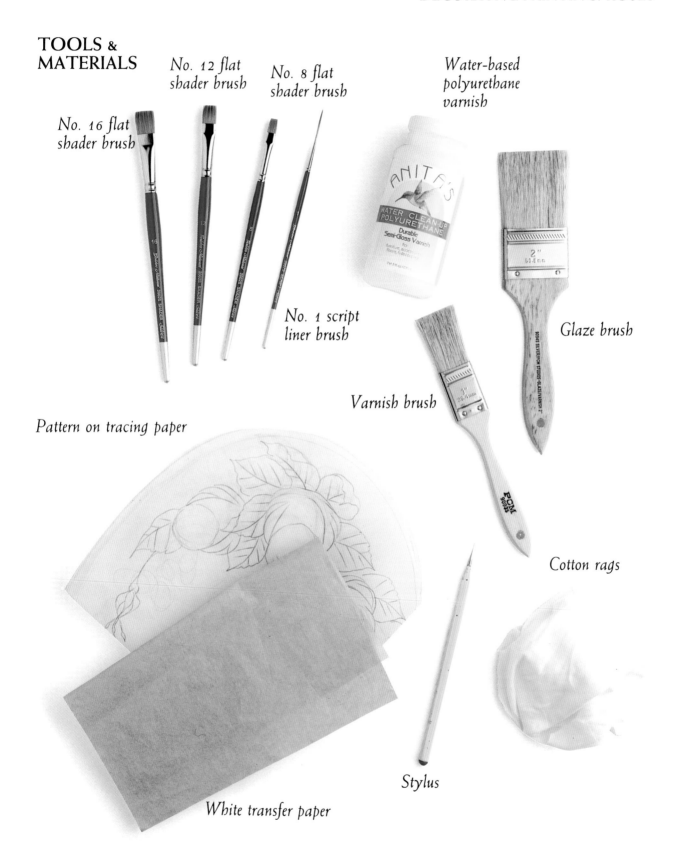

No. 16 flat
shader brush

No. 12 flat
shader brush

No. 8 flat
shader brush

Water-based
polyurethane
varnish

No. 1 script
liner brush

Glaze brush

Varnish brush

Pattern on tracing paper

Cotton rags

Stylus

White transfer paper

COLOR CHIPS—ARTIST'S ACRYLICS, WATER-BASED GLAZE

*Alizarin Crimson
  plus Burnt Umber
Alizarin Crimson
Rose Petal glaze
Cadmium Yellow
  Medium*

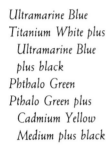   

*Ultramarine Blue
Titanium White plus
  Ultramarine Blue
  plus black
Phthalo Green
Pthalo Green plus
  Cadmium Yellow
  Medium plus black*

*Burnt Umber
Mars Black
Titanium White*

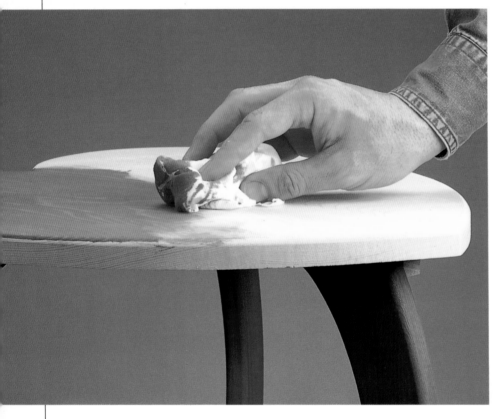

1 Using a glaze brush loaded with Rose Petal glaze, coat one section of the table at a time with color. Then, wipe and scrub color into the wood grain with a cotton rag. Remove excess glaze. If you wish a lighter background, wet a clean rag with water and wipe wood to remove some color. Let dry. To seal stain, brush on a coat of water-based polyurethane varnish with a varnish application brush.

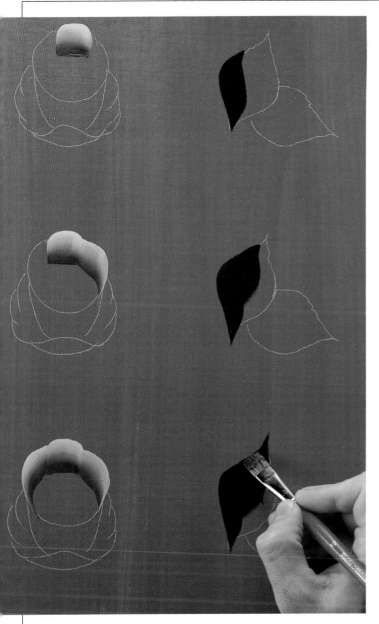

2 Trace and transfer rose design with tracing paper, white transfer paper and stylus. Base coat the leaves in a mixture of Phthalo Green plus Cadmium Yellow Medium plus black using a no. 12 flat shader brush. Create two values of burnt pink (light and dark) out of Alizarin Crimson plus Burnt Umber plus Titanium White. Double load a no. 16 flat shader brush with the light and dark pink mixtures to begin stroking on the back of the rose. (For a step-by-step demonstration of these decorative painting techniques, see page 22.)

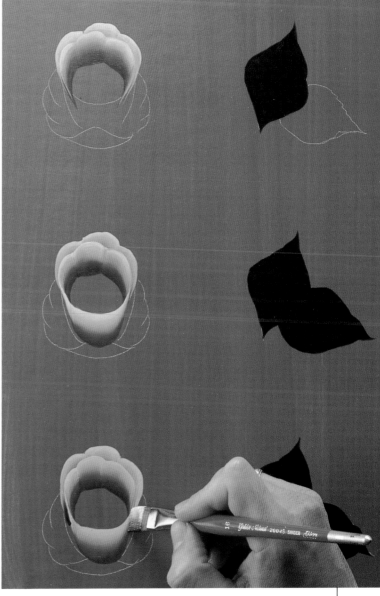

3 After the back petals of the rose have been stroked, you'll connect these petals to the front bowl of the rose by placing on a U stroke with the double-loaded brush. Place two bowl strokes, one over another, dropping the second one slightly.

4 Double load a no. 16 flat brush with the two pink mixtures and begin stroking on the rose's side petals. Shade the leaves with a side-loaded no. 12 flat brush of Mars Black. Place black at the base of the leaf and down the center vein. Pat blend out from the center vein with the black forming individual vein sections on one side.

Next, side load the no. 12 flat brush with ice mixture (Titanium White plus Ultramarine Blue plus black) and pat blend individual vein sections on the opposite side of the main center vein.

5 To highlight the leaves, side load the no. 12 flat brush with ice blue mixture and pat blend from the outside edge of the vein section in toward the center vein. Add accents on the edge of the leaves with a side-loaded no. 8 flat brush with the dark pink mixture. Draw fine vein lines with thin-consistency ice blue mix and the liner brush. Complete rose structure with the double-loaded no. 16 flat brush with the two values of pink.

Create a scalloped arc stroke for the back of the rose.

Paint two comma strokes on either side of the arc stroke.

Repeat steps, stroking on a second layer of petals slightly lower.

Create the first bowl of the rose using a U stroke.

Drop a second bowl of the rose lower, stroking on another U stroke.

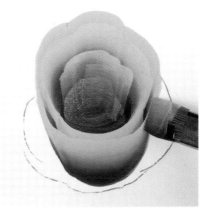

Fill in the throat of the rose by patting the brush upward. Restroke bowl.

Develop side petals by stroking on sliced comma strokes.

Add lower level of side petals with smaller slicelike comma strokes.

Add center lower petal by stroking on a "lazy" S stroke.

TEXTURIZING: PARCHMENT LOOK

Photo of detail on parchment-look table.

The look of old parchment paper is duplicated by the layering of a series of earth tone transparent colored glazes. These glazes are mottled with household plastic wrap to create the irregular tonal qualities found on real parchment paper. This pattern can be reproduced in a subtle approach with a majority of the markings blended away, or the markings from the plastic wrap can be kept sharp for a textured effect. This technique looks warm and handsome when it is combined with stained wood. Here, an inset panel is painted with the parchment technique trimmed in black bands and gold lines and surrounded by red-brown natural stain. ৯৯

TEXTURIZING: PARCHMENT LOOK

TOOLS & MATERIALS

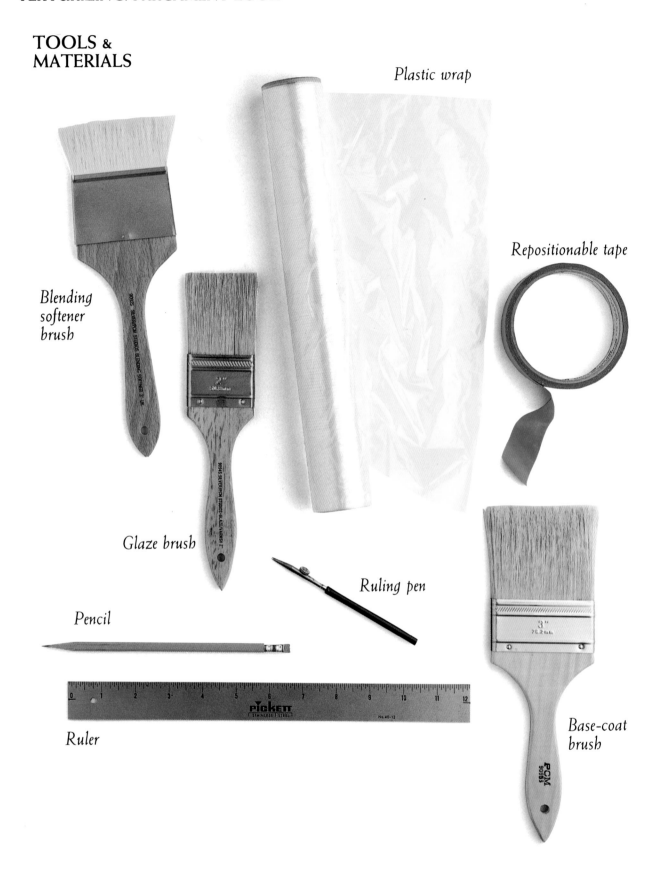

Plastic wrap

Repositionable tape

Blending
softener
brush

Glaze brush

Ruling pen

Pencil

Base-coat
brush

Ruler

COLOR CHIPS—WATER-BASED GLAZES, ARTIST'S ACRYLICS

Indian Brown glaze
Butter Cream glaze
Metallic Gold
  acrylic
Yellow Ochre
  acrylic

Dark Brown glaze
Mars Black acrylic
White glaze

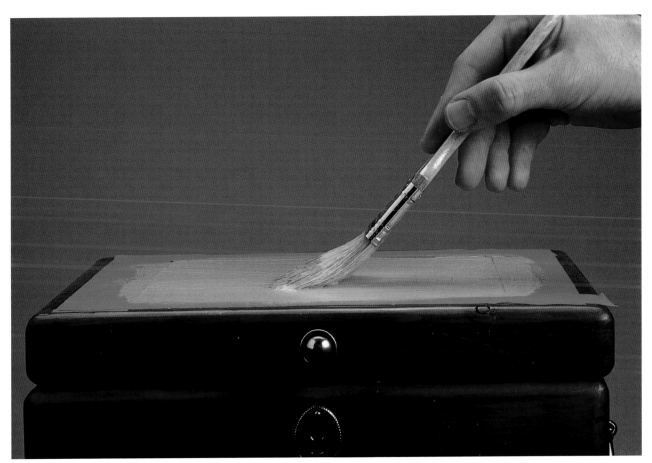

1 Measure and mark an inset panel on the stained tabletop with pencil and
ruler. Tape off the center inset panel section with repositionable tape.
Rub down the tape edge you'll be painting against with your fingernail or
credit card. Using a base-coat brush, apply several coats of Yellow Ochre
acrylic until an opaque coverage is achieved.

TEXTURIZING: PARCHMENT LOOK

2 Brush Dark Brown glaze over the Yellow Ochre base using a glaze application brush. Tear off a sheet of plastic wrap (slightly larger than area to be covered) and press the plastic wrap into the wet glaze. Be sure to create a lot of small creases in the plastic wrap to form a fine pattern. Pull plastic wrap off the surface and allow to dry thoroughly.

3 Coat the inset panel with Indian Brown glaze with a glaze application brsuh. Once again, tear off a piece of plastic wrap and press into the wet glaze to form a fine pattern. Pull plastic wrap off the surface and let dry.

4 Coat the inset panel with Butter Cream glaze with a glaze application brush. Tear off another piece of plastic wrap and press into wet glaze to form a fine network of creases. Pull plastic wrap off surface and allow to dry.

5 Coat the surface with white glaze with glaze brush, press a fresh piece of plastic wrap into the wet glaze and remove plastic wrap. While the white glaze is still wet, brush the surface lightly with a blending softener brush. Hold the brush upright and in a swiping motion dust the surface to blend some of the plastic wrap markings. You can blend as little or as much as you desire. Trim inset panel with black bands and gold lines using ruling pen.

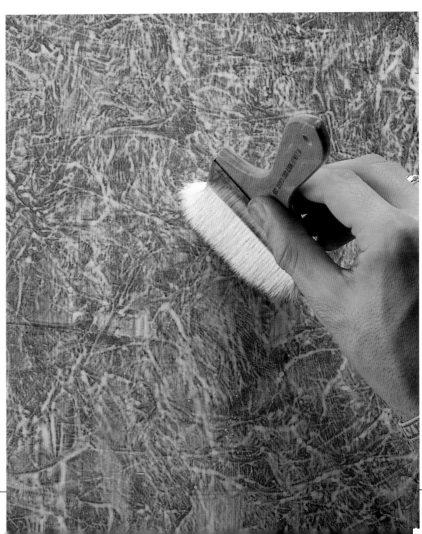

STROKE ART PAINTING: FLORALS

Photo of detail on stroke art floral table.

This loose, casual style of painting is a modern version of European folk art painting. The brush is loaded with multiple colors at a time and then fluid brushstrokes are executed to create a flower petal or leaf. There is no traditional blending method (dry brush blending or pat blending) of colors on the surface. The colors literally blend and mingle together as the pressure is applied to make the strokes that form the subject matter. This technique is ideal for a decorative painting novice. Since no blending skills are required, all you need to learn is proper brush loading and brushstroke control. ✺

TOOLS & MATERIALS

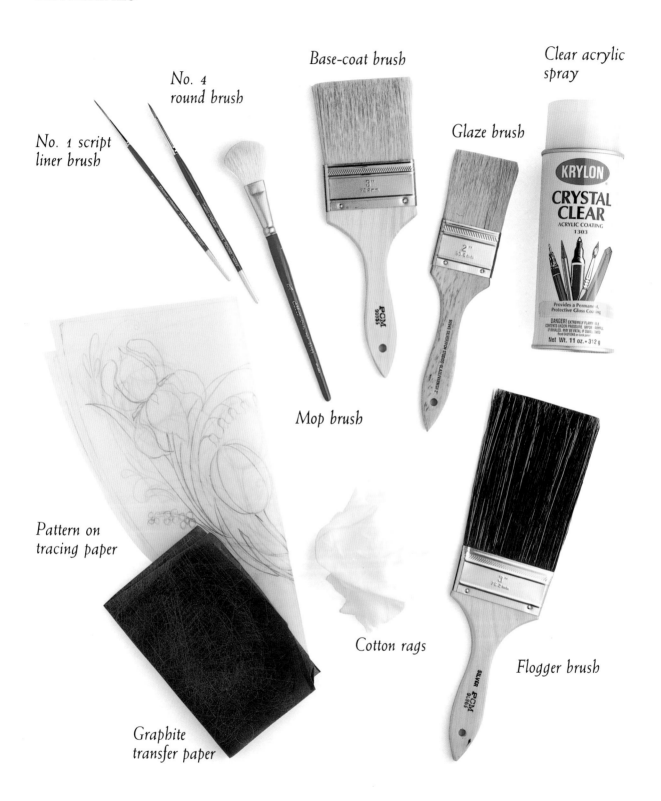

No. 4
round brush

Base-coat brush

Clear acrylic
spray

No. 1 script
liner brush

Glaze brush

Mop brush

Pattern on
tracing paper

Cotton rags

Flogger brush

Graphite
transfer paper

COLOR CHIPS—ARTIST'S ACRYLICS, WATER-BASED GLAZE, LATEX PAINT

Alizarin Crimson
Iridescent White plus
* Alizarin Crimson*
Iridescent Gold
Cadmium Yellow
* Medium*

Dioxazine Purple
Ultramarine Blue
Ultramarine Blue
* plus black*
Iridescent White plus
* Dioxazine Purple*
* plus Ultramarine*
* Blue*

Mars Back
Phthalo Green plus
* black*
Burnt Umber
Burnt Sienna

Periwinkle Blue
* semigloss latex*
* paint*
Titanium White plus
* Burnt Umber*
Butter Cream glaze
Iridescent White

Titanium White

1 Base coat the tabletop with several coats of Periwinkle Blue semigloss latex paint using a base-coat application brush. Let dry. Create a strie finish using Butter Cream glaze and a flogger brush. Let dry. Seal and protect the strie finish with several light mistings of clear acrylic spray. Trace and transfer the design using tracing paper and graphite transfer paper.

STROKE ART PAINTING: FLORALS

2 Create all the paint mixtures and then thin all acrylic colors with water to a thin, creamy consistency. Load a no. 4 round brush with Phthalo Green plus black thoroughly saturating all the brush's hairs. Now, tip the brush's point into the pile of Iridescent Gold. To paint the leaf blades and stems, stroke the round brush in one long, fluid stroke. Turn and twist the brush to form rolling-over leaf blades. Add a few comma-stroke, loose leaf forms.

3 To paint the tulips, saturate the round brush first with Iridescent White plus Alizarin Crimson, then stroke through the pile of Cadmium Yellow Medium and tip the point of the brush in Titanium White. Stroke on the side petals forming flat commas. Paint the center tulip petal in three commas—two curving side strokes and one center straight comma. Load the brush with fresh colors as needed. Base coat the blossoms with circle strokes of Titanium White plus Burnt Umber.

To paint iris, load round brush with Ultramarine Blue plus Mars Black, stroke through Dioxazine Purple and tip the brush in Iridescent White. Stroke the iris with multiple comma strokes.

4 To paint the blossom flowers, load the round brush with Alizarin Crimson, stroke through Iridescent White plus Alizarin Crimson and tip the brush in Titanium White. Stroke on four pull strokes (comma stroke without tail). Dab in blossom center with Cadmium Yellow Medium and Burnt Sienna. Bluebells are stroked on with the round brush loaded with Iridescent White plus Dioxazine Purple plus Ultramarine Blue and tipped in Iridescent White.

5 Finish with loose scrolls painted with thin-consistency Phthalo Green plus black and a liner brush. Add any additional embellishment and let dry. Seal painting with several mistings of clear acrylic spray.

A "ghost" glaze can be placed over the painting to soften. Brush on Butter Cream glaze with glaze application brush, then wipe off desired amount with a cotton rag and soften with mop brush.

JEWEL APPLICATION: GLAMOUR LOOK

Photo of detail on glamour-look table.

The addition of jewel stones and glitter to the table creates an "over the top" approach. This look is perfect for a modern decorating scheme where bright, high chroma colors are being employed. This table could also be used in a young child's bedroom for a playful circus quality. The combination of iridescent acrylic colors, metallic gold and glitter add to the dazzling effect of the *faux* gemstones. You can create a structured graphic approach as illustrated here or complete a freestyle approach where the gemstones are placed in a scattered manner. Whatever your approach, this table will be eye-catching. ❧

TOOLS & MATERIALS

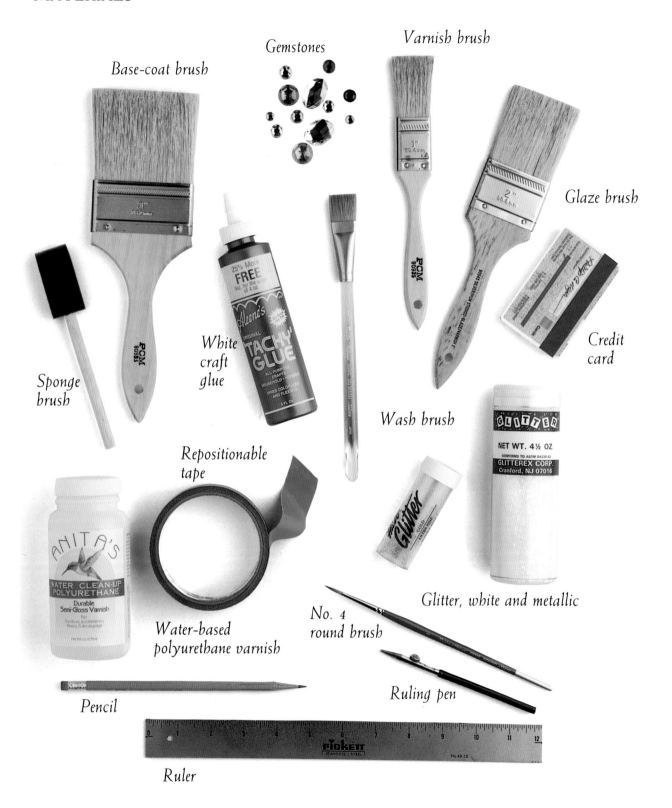

Base-coat brush

Gemstones

Varnish brush

Glaze brush

White craft glue

Credit card

Sponge brush

Wash brush

Repositionable tape

Glitter, white and metallic

Water-based polyurethane varnish

No. 4 round brush

Pencil

Ruling pen

Ruler

COLOR CHIPS—ARTIST'S ACRYLICS

Iridescent Red
Iridescent Gold
Iridescent Blue
Iridescent Purple

Iridescent Green
Mars Black

1 Base coat the table with Iridescent Gold using a base-coat application brush. Apply four to five coats to achieve an opaque coverage. (Note: This table features a center inset of white ceramic tile.) Let base coat cure thoroughly before proceeding.

JEWEL APPLICATION: GLAMOUR LOOK

2 Measure and mark inset panels using the pencil and ruler. Place panels three-quarters of an inch to a full inch (1.9cm to 2.5cm) from all edges. Mask these areas off with re-positionable tape and burnish tape with a credit card.

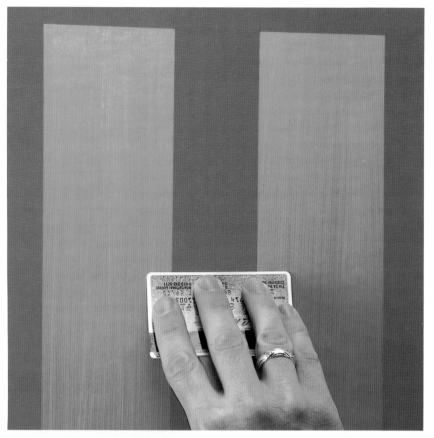

3 Paint inset panels in alternating iridescent colors of your choice. Apply paint as smoothly as possible using a sponge brush or glaze brush. It will take four to five coats to achieve an opaque coverage with iridescent colors. Allow to dry thoroughly.

4 To determine gemstone placement, pick up individual stones and set in a variety of layouts. Take the time to work out a graphic grid structure or a loose, scattered placement. Make a mental note of the overall placement of stones.

5 Apply white craft glue to the surface with a no. 4 round brush and press each gemstone in place. After all stones are in place, clean up excess glue with a wash brush moistened with clean water. Let dry. Trim out inset panel with fine line of black using the ruling pen and thin-consistency Mars Black.

To add sparkling highlights to the table, coat the table with water-based polyurethane varnish using a varnish brush. While the varnish is still wet, sprinkle the table with a combination of white and metallic glitter.

FOLK ART PAINTING: FRUITS

Photo of detail of Folk Art fruit table.

The fruit painted on this table was developed in a colorful folk art approach. The subjects were rendered with shading and highlights to represent dimensional forms but are not meant to allude to a realistic still life. The deep background tones of the Forest Green stain create a striking dark contrast to the fruit painting. A light antiquing over the entire table helps tie in all the colors and tones down some of the color brightness. This table would be a great addition to a kitchen or breakfast room. ❧

TOOLS & MATERIALS

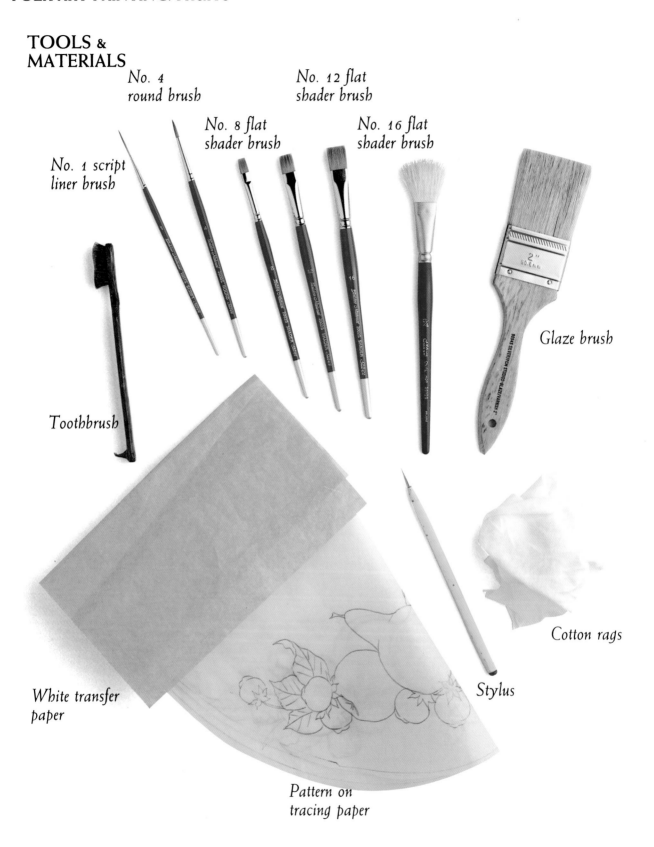

No. 4
round brush

No. 12 flat
shader brush

No. 8 flat
shader brush

No. 16 flat
shader brush

No. 1 script
liner brush

Glaze brush

Toothbrush

Cotton rags

White transfer
paper

Stylus

Pattern on
tracing paper

COLOR CHIPS—ARTIST'S ACRYLICS, WATER-BASED GLAZES

Alizarin Crimson
Bright Red
Cadmium Red Light
Cadmium Yellow
*   Medium*

Ultramarine Blue
Phthalo Green plus
*   Ultramarine Blue*
*   plus black*
Phthalo Green
Forest Green glaze

Alizarin Crimson
*   plus Burnt Umber*
Burnt Umber
Burnt Sienna
Yellow Ochre

Mars Black
Titanium White
Dark Brown glaze
Indian Brown glaze

1 Stain the table with Forest Green glaze. Brush the glaze on a section of the table at a time with a glaze application brush. Remove excess glaze with a cotton rag. To highlight the wood grain and lighten up any dark areas, moisten a fresh cotton rag with water and wipe away some of the glaze. Let dry.

2 Trace and transfer the fruit design using tracing paper and white transfer paper. Base coat the pears and peaches in Yellow Ochre using a no. 16 flat brush. Base the apples and strawberries in Bright Red using a No. 12 flat brush. Apply several coats until opaque. Side load the no. 16 flat brush with Alizarin Crimson plus Burnt Umber and shade the apples and strawberries. (For step-by-step demonstrations of decorative painting techniques, see page 21.)

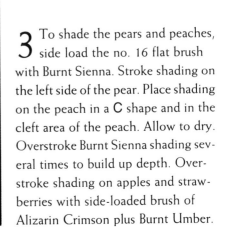

3 To shade the pears and peaches, side load the no. 16 flat brush with Burnt Sienna. Stroke shading on the left side of the pear. Place shading on the peach in a **C** shape and in the cleft area of the peach. Allow to dry. Overstroke Burnt Sienna shading several times to build up depth. Overstroke shading on apples and strawberries with side-loaded brush of Alizarin Crimson plus Burnt Umber.

FOLK ART PAINTING: FRUITS

4 Dry brush highlights on the peach with a no. 12 flat brush and Yellow Ochre. Drag brush over surface with dry color. To begin building highlights on all fruits, side load a no. 8 flat brush with Cadmium Yellow Medium. Stroke this in a circular direction. Add seed pockets on strawberries using a no. 4 round brush and Alizarin Crimson plus Burnt Umber. Add color streaks of thin-consistency Cadmium Red Light and Cadmium Yellow Medium using a liner brush.

5 Flyspeck the pear with thin-consistency Burnt Sienna and a toothbrush. Paint fruit stems with Burnt Umber and highlight with dabs of white using no. 4 round brush. Base all leaves and strawberry calyx with a mixture of Phthalo Green plus Ultramarine Blue plus black using no. 8 flat shader brush. Apply second coat and while still wet add Cadmium Yellow Medium to blend in a highlight. Next, pick up white on the "dirty" brush and stroke on a stronger highlight area. Add vein on leaves with liner brush and "dirty" white (white plus green). Add sharper highlight with a no. 12 flat brush side loaded with white. Antique table using Dark Brown and Indian Brown glazes. Brush on glazes with glaze brush, wipe off excess with cotton rags and soften with mop brush.

Phillip C. Wylie

Phillip C. Myer

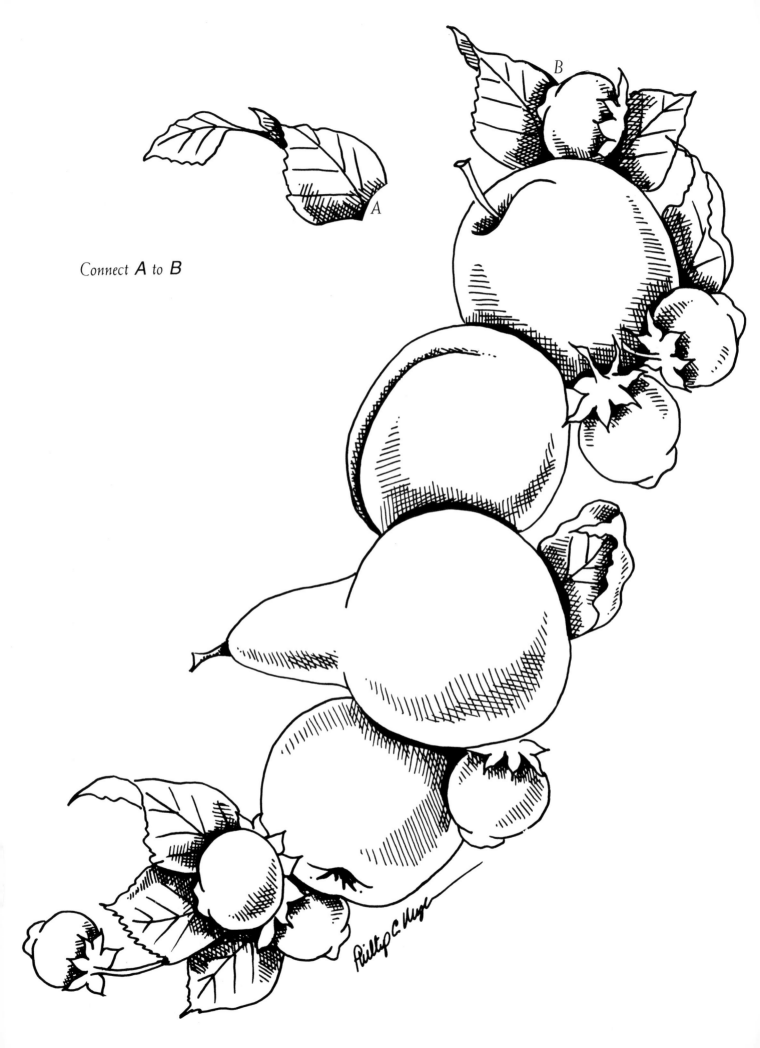

Connect *A* to *B*

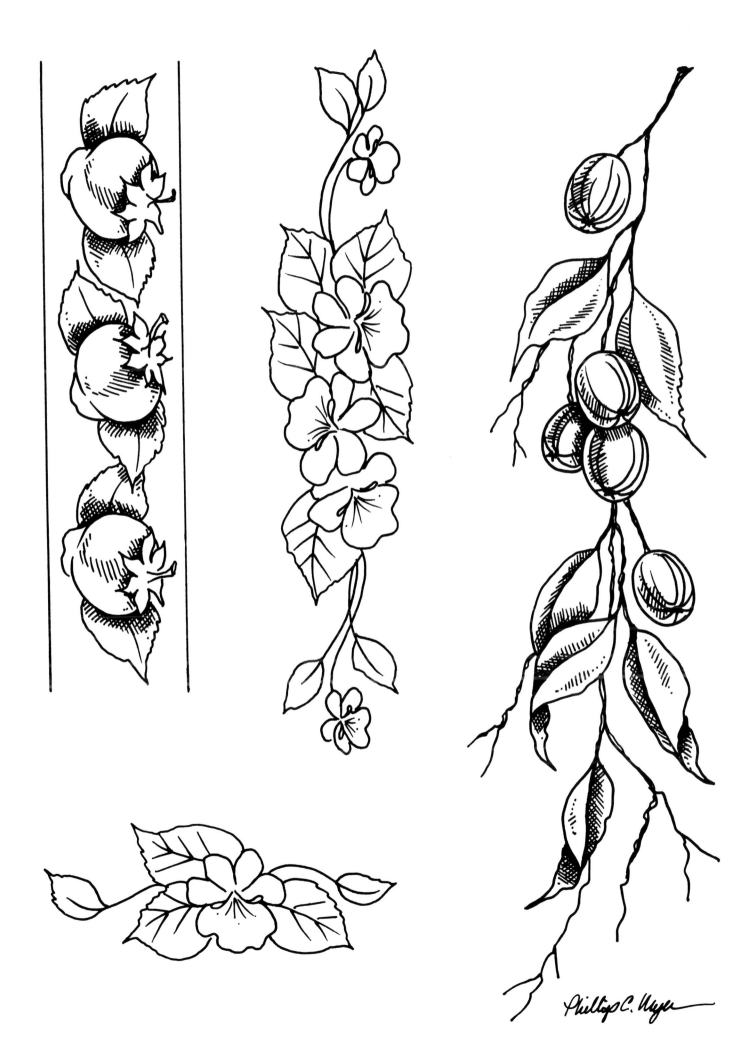

Phillips C. Meyer

GLOSSARY

ACRYLIC POLYMER—a thermoplastic resin, with a synthetic substance or mixture, used as a binder with powdered pigments in the creation of artist's acrylic colors.

ANTIQUING—the application of a very thin, transparent coating placed over a surface to provide the illusion of age and patina.

ARTIST'S ACRYLIC COLORS—paint that is a mixture of powdered pigments ground in thermoplastic, synthetic emulsions. They can be thinned and cleaned up with water.

BASE COAT—the initial application of paint to a surface.

BODY—the weight or form of an object; as it relates to paint, the consistency can carry a form or volume.

BURNISH—to polish, or to rub a surface with a hard tool, especially to adhere and smooth areas.

CHISEL—the sharp edge that forms on the end of a well-crafted flat brush.

COLOR VALUES—the degrees of lightness, darkness, saturation and brightness of a hue.

CRACKLED—when a surface shows random separations in its paint or varnish finish, making it appear older than it really is; can result from product incompatibility, temperature or weather.

CRISSCROSS—a paint stroke direction that forms crossed lines, overlapping randomly, making X shapes.

CURTAINING—the sagging or dripping of a layer of paint or varnish that has been placed over a previous coat that is not cured and dried; the top layer weights down the first layer that is not dried and pulls both layers down like a sagging "curtain."

DARK VALUE—the deeper color tones on the gray scale that can be created from any color by the addition of its color complement or black.

DECORATIVE PAINTING—an ornamental art form used to decorate functional as well as nonfunctional surfaces; it is a teachable art form broken down into step-by-step methods.

DECOUPAGE—the French art form of cutting and pasting down images to form decorative treatments on a surface.

DISTRESSING—the action of battering a surface through the use of abrasive tools such as sandpaper, hammer, nail, screw or chains; the goal is to imitate age and the wear and tear of a surface.

DOUBLE LOAD—to carry two colors on a brush at one time, side by side, with a smooth gradation between.

EARTH TONES—colors that are made with natural pigments (like yellow ochre, which is made from refined clay).

FAUX—the French word which translates as *false* or *fake*; as it relates to painted finishes, it defines a painted look that mimics a real surface: *faux marble*—painted to look like marble; *faux bois*—painted to look like wood grain.

FLAT—as it relates to paint, the sheen or finish that is dull and porous.

FLECKS—small particles of paint spattered on the surface.

FLYSPECKING—the painting technique that disperses small particles of thin-consistency paint over the surface with the use of a toothbrush.

FREEHAND—to create without the use of patterns or guidelines.

GLAZE—a transparent mixture of color plus a clear painting medium.

GLOSS—the highest level of a finish's sheen or shine qualities.

GRAY SCALE—a standardized chart of values from white to black (from lightest to darkest) in percentage increments.

GRID—a framed structure of equally spaced parallel bars and crossbars used to paint various tile or stripe patterns. A grid is also used to enlarge or reduce the size of designs by scaling them up or down proportionately.

HAZE—a transparent but cloudy or smoky coating over a surface that obstructs the clarity of the color below.

HIGH CONTRAST—an extreme color value difference in close proximity; the highest level would be from white to gray to black in a short distance.

HUE—the quality of color; the intensity of color, as in a shade or tint.

INKLIKE CONSISTENCY—paint thinned with painting medium, painting glaze or solvent to the liquid state that matches drawing ink.

LATEX—paint made from powdered pigments ground with emulsion of rubber or plastic globules. It can be cleaned with water.

LIFT-OFF—the intentional or accidental removal of base coat, paint finish or varnish.

LIGHT VALUE—the brighter color values on the gray scale. Any color can become a light value by the addition of white.

MASKING—to mark off an area and then protect that area by covering with tape or other items so that it won't receive paint when a nearby area is being painted.

MEDIUM—the type of paint used, such as acrylics or oils; or a liquid, such as water-based varnish, acrylic retarder and water, used to thin acrylic paints.

MEDIUM VALUE—a color tone that is simply not too dark and not too light; a shade in the middle from dark value to light value.

MIDTONE—a center point of a color's value in relation to its lightest or darkest points within a given painted area.

MONTAGE—to overlap design elements on a surface until very little or nothing of the original surface shows; a technique employed in decoupage.

MULTITONE—the development of a variety of values of one color or many colors on a surface.

OPAQUE—paint coverage that is thick enough so that light cannot pass through it.

OPEN TIME—the period in which the paints, painting mediums or varnishes will remain workable before they begin to set up and dry.

PAINT RUNS—usually undesirable drips of paint or varnish that move down a vertical surface.

PASTE WAX—a coating of specially designed wax that is rubbed on and adds a level of polish and sheen to a surface.

PATINA—the marks and signs of aging that develop on a surface creating character often thought of as patina; the corrosion that occurs as metals oxidize.

PATTERN—a guideline to follow when creating, as in woodworking, sewing or decorative painting.

POROUS—relating to a surface with permeable openings that moisture easily penetrates.

PRIMER—an opaque, paintlike basecoat application that seals the surface and readies it for decorative treatment; a stain-blocking sealer that does not allow bottom coats to penetrate through.

RETARDER—an agent that suspends and slows down the quick drying time

of some water-based products such as acrylics.

RULING—the painted fine line trim work through the application of thin-consistency paint with a ruling pen.

SAGGING—the lifting and dropping of a coat of paint due to improper surface preparation.

SATIN—a step up from a flat finish; a surface with a slight amount of sheen or shine.

SEMIGLOSS—a surface with a sheen level greater than satin but less than gloss.

SETUP TIME—the period it takes for the paint, painting glaze or varnish to begin to dry and become tacky.

SIDE LOAD—to carry color only on one side of the brush with painting medium or solvent on the other, creating a blended transition on the brush from opaque color to transparent color to no color.

SOLVENT—the agent that cleans and thins paint and varnishes and acts as a painting medium. A paint's solvent can be used as a painting medium; the solvent for acrylic is water, the solvent for oils is turpentine.

STRIE—the painted finish technique that creates irregular linear streaks in a wet paint glaze through the use of a flogger brush.

STRIPING—the addition of horizontal or vertical lines (or a combination of both) in any degree of line width.

STRIPPING—the removal of paint, varnish or other buildup on a surface through the use of commercially made chemical products and scraping tools.

TACKY—a sticky quality that develops during the drying time of a paint product. Some techniques require waiting for a tacky paint/glue/varnish/state before proceeding with the technique.

TELEGRAPHING—the action of an impression or pattern coming up from a foundation level, exposing itself to the

top layers that were placed over it to hide it or cover it up.

THICK, CREAMY CONSISTENCY—a paint mixed with a very small amount of painting medium, paint glaze or solvent, whipped to the texture of whipped butter; paint should hold peaks when patted with palette knife.

THIN, CREAMY CONSISTENCY—a paint mixed with painting medium, paint glaze or solvent, whipped to the texture of whipped cream.

THIN, SOUPY CONSISTENCY—a paint mixed with painting medium, paint glaze or solvent to the texture of watered-down soup.

TONAL AND GRADATION—the creation of various color tones that intermingle and go down the gray scale in an even transition:

TONE ON TONE—the layering of subtle color values very close in lightness or darkness on the gray scale.

TRANSPARENT—relating to a coating of paint or glaze so thin that light can easily pass through; when something is transparent, you can see through it clearly.

VALUE—the ratio or percentage of color that relates to the gray scale; a color from lightest to darkest.

VARNISH—a clear coating of either a polyurethane-based or water- or oil-based product that protects what is underneath the coating.

VEINS—the interior structural pattern element found in leaf structures.

WASH—paint thinned with enough painting medium, paint glaze or solvent to make it fluid and transparent.

WOOD GRAIN—the pattern of marks found in wood surfaces; a flowing organic pattern.

WOOD PUTTY—the thick compound made of whiting, linseed oil and binders in a dough-like consistency, used to fill imperfections on a wood surface before painting or finishing.

SOURCES

*T*he following companies are manufacturers, mail order suppliers of the specific materials used to create the decorated tables found in this book. Also listed are facilities that offer instructional materials or seminars. Write for further information. Provide a stamped, self-addressed return envelope for a response.

BRUSHES
Silver Brush Limited
92 N. Main St., Bldg. 18C
Windsor, NJ 08561
(609) 443-4900 Phone
(609) 443-4888 Fax

GLAZES, GLUES & VARNISHES
Back Street, Inc.
3905 Steve Reynolds Blvd.
Norcross, GA 30093
(770) 381-7373 Phone
(770) 381-6424 Fax

PAINTS—PRIMA ARTIST'S ACRYLICS
Martin/F. Weber Co.
2727 Southampton Rd.
Philadelphia, PA 19154
(215) 677-5600 Phone
(215) 677-3336 Fax

TAPES
3M Consumer Products Group
P.O. Box 33053
St. Paul, MN 55133
(612) 733-1110 Phone

UNFINISHED TABLES
The following companies produce the unfinished tables decorated in this book:

- Distressing—Wax Technique
- Pen-and-Ink Color Wash—Violets

Artcraft Wood Etc.
415 E. Seventh St.
Joplin, MO 64801
(417) 782-7063 Phone
(417) 782-7064 Fax

- Decorative Painting—Strawberries
J.B. Wood Products
P.O. Box 3084
South Attleboro, MA 02703
(508) 226-3217 Phone
(508) 222-9399 Fax

- Decoupage—Vegetable Print
- Tole Painting—Pennsylvania Dutch
- Decorative Painting—Gooseberries
- Stroke Art Painting—Florals
Target Corp.
33 S. Sixth St.
Minneapolis, MN 55402
(612) 304-6073 Phone
(800) 800-8800 Phone—for the store near you.

- Texturizing—Parchment Look
Two Day Designs
Route 1, Box 162-A
Eastanollee, GA 30538
(706) 779-5485 Phone
(706) 779-5485 Fax

- Jewel Application—Glamour Look
Wal-Mart
702 SW Eighth St.

Bentonville, AR 72716
(501) 278-4000

- Decorative Painting—Roses
- Folk Art Painting—Fruits
Walnut Hollow
Route 1
Dodgeville, WI 53533
(608) 935-2341 Phone
(608) 935-3029 Fax

- Strie—Linear Finish
- Spray Texture—Pottery Finish
- Ceramic Application—Broken Tile
Whittier Wood Products
P.O. Box 2827
Eugene, OR 97402
(541) 687-0213 Phone

SCHOOLS
The following are schools that specialize in the teaching of paint and faux finishes for the decoration of accessories, furniture and interiors:

American Academy of Decorative Finishes
14255 N. Seventy-Nineth St., Suite 10
Scottsdale, AZ 85260
(602) 991-8560 Phone
(602) 991-9779 Fax

Day Studio Workshop, Inc.
1504 Bryant St.
San Francisco, CA 94103
(415) 626-9300 Phone

Finishing School, Inc.
334 Main St.
Port Washington, NY 11050
(516) 767-6422 Phone
(516) 767-7406 Fax

PCM Studios
School of the Decorative Arts
731 Highland Ave. NE, Suite D
Atlanta, GA 30312
(404) 222-0348 Phone
(404) 222-0348 Fax

INDEX